WOMEN WHO DARE

Women Explorers

BY SHARON M. HANNON

*Jean: I hope you enjoy these stories
about these amazing women.*

Sharon M. Hannon

Pomegranate

SAN FRANCISCO

LIBRARY OF CONGRESS
WASHINGTON, DC

Published by Pomegranate Communications, Inc.
Box 808022, Petaluma CA 94975
800 227 1428; www.pomegranate.com

Pomegranate Europe Ltd.
Unit 1, Heathcote Business Centre, Hurlbutt Road
Warwick, Warwickshire CV34 6TD, UK
[+44] 0 1926 430111; sales@pomeurope.co.uk

Amy Pastan, Series Editor

In association with the Library of Congress, Pomegranate publishes other books in the Women Who Dare® series, as well as calendars, books of postcards, posters, and Knowledge Cards® featuring daring women. Please contact the publisher for more information.

Library of Congress Cataloging-in-Publication Data

Hannon, Sharon M.
     Women who dare : women explorers / by Sharon M. Hannon.
         p. cm.
     Includes bibliographical references.
     ISBN-13: 978-0-7649-3892-4
     1. Women explorers—Biography. I. Title.

  G200.H27 2007
  910.92'2—dc22

                                        2006050706

Pomegranate Catalog No. A134
Designed by Harrah Lord, Yellow House Studio, Rockport, ME
Printed in Korea

16 15 14 13 12 11 10 09 08 07   10 9 8 7 6 5 4 3 2 1

FRONT COVER: *Harriet Chalmers Adams traveling by camel through the Gobi Desert in Mongolia.*
CPH 3B43526
BACK COVER: *Constanza Ceruti climbing Aconcagua.* COURTESY CONSTANZA CERUTI

PREFACE

FOR TWO HUNDRED YEARS, the Library of Congress, the oldest national cultural institution in the United States, has been gathering materials necessary to tell the stories of women in America. The last third of the twentieth century witnessed a great surge of popular and scholarly interest in women's studies and women's history that has led to an outpouring of works in many formats. Drawing on women's history resources in the collections of the Library of Congress, the Women Who Dare book series is designed to provide readers with an entertaining introduction to the life of a notable American woman or a significant topic in women's history.

From its beginnings in 1800 as a legislative library, the Library of Congress has grown into a national library that houses both a universal collection of knowledge and the mint record of American creativity. Congress' decision to purchase Thomas Jefferson's personal library to replace the books and maps burned during the British occupation in 1814 set the Congressional Library on the path of collecting with the breadth of Jefferson's interests. Not just American imprints were to be acquired, but foreign-language materials as well, and Jefferson's library already included works by American and European women.

The Library of Congress has some 121 million items, largely housed in closed stacks in three buildings on Capitol Hill that contain twenty public reading rooms. The incredible, wide-ranging collections include books, maps, prints, newspapers, broadsides, diaries, letters, posters, musical scores, photographs, audio and video recordings, and documents available only in digital formats. The Library serves first-time users and the most experienced researchers alike.

I hope that you, the reader, will seek and find in the pages of this book information that will further your understanding of women's history. In addition, I hope you will continue to explore the topic of this book in a library near you, in person at the Library of Congress, or by visiting the Library on the World Wide Web at http://www.loc.gov. Happy reading!

—JAMES H. BILLINGTON, The Librarian of Congress

To those bred under an elaborate social order few such moments of exhilaration can come as that which stands at the threshold of wild travel. The gates of the enclosed garden are thrown open, the chain at the entrance of the sanctuary is lowered, with a wary glance to the right and left you step forth, and, behold! the immeasurable world.

—Gertrude Bell, the opening lines of
The Desert and the Sown (1907)

I n the mid-nineteenth century, a few intrepid women began leaving their homes in Europe and North America to travel alone to far-off lands. Unlike earlier women who had journeyed as missionaries or migrated for social or religious reasons, these women were not driven by any particular cause. Their innate curiosity to explore the people and places they had read about, and the sense of freedom they found when traveling, drove them on despite the difficulties and criticism they faced as solo women travelers. On the road for months and years at a time, they wrote vivid accounts of their adventures, which sold well to a public obsessed with tales of the exotic.

■ *British explorer Gertrude Bell (1868–1926), seen here between Winston Churchill and T. E. Lawrence (Lawrence of Arabia), was a recognized authority on the Middle East. Recruited by the British Arab Intelligence Bureau on the eve of World War I, she was later the only woman to participate in Churchill's committee to determine the fate of the region. Bell was instrumental in the creation of the modern state of Iraq and founded the Iraq Museum in Baghdad a few years before her death.*

PHOTOGRAPH COURTESY UNIVERSITY OF NEWCASTLE UPON TYNE

Initially these women were self-effacing—an approach acceptable to Victorian society—and did not view themselves as explorers or scientists on par with men. In *Travels in West Africa* (1897), British explorer Mary Kingsley began, "What this book wants is not a simple Preface but an apology, and a very brilliant and convincing one at that." Still, they were often criticized as vain, a most unladylike characteristic. Why else would a woman want to wander about the world, writing of her experiences?

But society's attitudes toward these women would change—slowly. Books by Victorian-era "lady travelers," as the press referred to them, continued to sell well, and their authors were asked to lecture and write articles. Some eventually received small grants from their governments or museums to fund further exploration, although nothing like the huge sums given to male explorers.

By the first decade of the twentieth century, women were breaking mountain climbing records in Bolivia and Kashmir; cycling across India; traveling by camel through the Middle East, yak through Asia, and mule pack through the Andes; and collecting anthropological information about the women and children they met. They were photographing the wonders they saw and changing the way their societies looked at women and the world.

HERE, THERE, AND EVERYWHERE
WOMEN EXPLORE THE WORLD

IDA REYER PFEIFFER (1797–1858)

I had found by experience, that a woman of an energetic mind can find her way through the world as well as a man, and that good people are to be met with every where.

—Ida Pfeiffer, from *Visit to Iceland and the Scandinavian North* (1852)

WHEN FORTY-FIVE-YEAR-OLD HOUSEWIFE and mother Ida Pfeiffer set out on her own in the 1840s to visit the places she had always longed to see, she was a woman without role models. But her determination and drive in the final sixteen years of her life transformed her into a world traveler and best-selling author, earning her membership in the geographical societies of Berlin and Paris.

In Vienna, Austria, Ida Reyer's father had raised her to play outdoors and wear the same clothing as her five brothers. She had even received the same education as her siblings. At twenty-two, she married an older widower named Pfeiffer, a lawyer and government official. Within a few years, they had two sons but a difficult marriage, so after inheriting part of an estate, Ida Pfeiffer left her husband and returned to Vienna with her children. "When my sons' education had been completed, and I was living in peaceful retirement, the dreams and aspirations of my youth gradually awoke once more," she later wrote. "I thought of strange manners and customs, of distant regions, where a new sky would be above me, and new ground beneath my feet."

■ *To prepare for her visit to the Bataks, a tribe of cannibals in Sumatra, Ida Pfeiffer memorized a short speech, partly in Malay and partly in their language. Later, when she found herself surrounded by threatening, angry tribesmen, she told them that she was too old and tough and would not be good to eat—thereby escaping danger.* CPH 3C08109

■ *Throughout her long journeys, Ida Pfeiffer usually traveled alone and often lived with the indigenous people. Yet she always believed that the people of Christian Europe were superior to the "heathens, infidels, and savages" she encountered elsewhere.*

She began to plan a trip abroad. As a concession to her friends, she agreed to put her affairs in order before leaving. "I made my will, and arranged all my worldly affairs in such a manner that, in the case of my death (an event which I considered more probable than my safe return), my family should find everything perfectly arranged," she wrote. "And thus, on the 22nd of March 1842, I commenced my journey from Vienna." Her destination: the Holy Land.

For the next nine months, Pfeiffer visited Constantinople, Cairo, and Jerusalem, rode camels, climbed the pyramids, and visited the Great Sphinx. Upon returning home, she published her journal of the trip. *A Visit to the Holy Land, Egypt, and Italy* sold well, and she used the money to finance a trip to Iceland and Scandinavia in 1845. To raise more money, she wrote *Visit to Iceland and the Scandinavian North* and sold the rocks and plants she had collected to museums.

In May 1846 Pfeiffer began a nineteen-month trip around the world. Traveling by sailing ship, it took her two and one-half months just to cross the Atlantic. In Brazil she had her first experiences with indigenous peoples when she and her guide slashed through jungle to visit a tribe of Puri Indians and enjoyed a meal of roasted monkey and parrot.

Her book chronicling these adventures, *A Women's Journey Round the World,* made her an international celebrity, but despite offers of free passage and lodging, financing her trips remained a problem. Eventually, with a small grant from the Austrian government, she set off in 1851 on another trip around the world. She spent six months exploring the interior of Borneo, where she visited the Dyaks, a headhunter tribe, and encountered

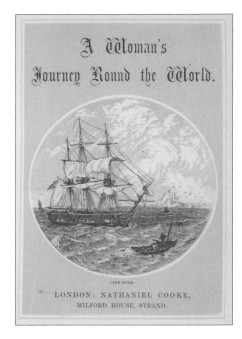

A Woman's
Journey Round the World.

CAPE HORN.

LONDON: NATHANIEL COOKE,
MILFORD HOUSE, STRAND.

■ *In* A Woman's Journey Round
the World, *Ida Pfeiffer described
her adventures from 1846 to 1848,
during which she dressed like a man
in China to walk around Canton
freely, joined a camel caravan in
Baghdad for a three-hundred-mile
journey across the desert to Mosul
and northern Persia, and spent a
night in a Russian jail when she
was mistaken for a spy.*
GENERAL COLLECTIONS,
LIBRARY OF CONGRESS

the Batak tribe of cannibals in Sumatra. After a four-year absence, Pfeiffer
returned home and wrote *A Woman's Second Journey Around the World,*
another best seller.

During her final trip, she was imprisoned in Madagascar for her
alleged involvement in a plot to overthrow the queen. By the time Pfeiffer
was released, she had contracted a tropical fever; she died in Vienna in
1858 at age sixty-one.

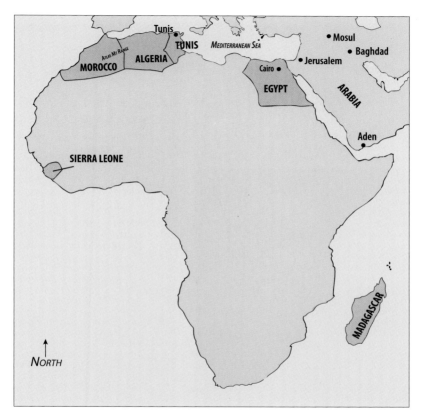

■ *Map of Africa, c. 1895, highlighting the countries and ancient cities of the Middle East and North Africa that were among the most popular destinations for women explorers, beginning with Ida Pfeiffer's 1842 trip to the Holy Land.* MAP DESIGNED BY STEPHANIE HELLINE

ISABELLA BIRD BISHOP (1831–1904)

GROWING UP IN NORTHERN ENGLAND, Isabella Bird was a sickly child. Heeding her doctor's advice to keep her outdoors as much as possible, her father taught her to ride horses and quizzed her about the plants, trees, and crops they passed. At eighteen she underwent surgery for a spinal tumor and for the rest of her life suffered from back pain and occasional depression. In 1854, her doctor suggested she take a sea voyage for her health, so in June she sailed to North America with two cousins.

Whether due to the open sea, fresh air, or change from her usual routine, her health improved dramatically. Seven months later she returned to England and, with her father's encouragement,

■ *The quintessential Victorian "lady traveler," Isabella Bird Bishop circled the globe three times and wrote nine books before she died at age seventy-two. She set a standard for women travelers that endured well into the twentieth century. In 1892 she became the first woman to become a member of and address the Royal Geographical Society.*

MID-MANHATTAN PICTURE COLLECTION, NEW YORK PUBLIC LIBRARY, ASTOR, LENOX, AND TILDEN FOUNDATIONS

wrote her first book, *The Englishwoman in America* (1856), which sold well and garnered favorable reviews on both sides of the Atlantic.

Sixteen years later, with both parents now deceased, she left her home in Edinburgh, Scotland, for Australia and New Zealand and spent seven months in the Sandwich Islands (now Hawaii) touring on horseback. It was here that she first rode astride rather than sidesaddle and began wearing Turkish trousers, though she covered them with a long skirt. In Estes Park, Colorado, she met Irish Canadian trapper and Indian scout "Mountain Jim" Nugent, who became one of the more intriguing figures in her life. She spent months riding, climbing, and camping with Mountain Jim in the Rockies. Her book *A Lady's Life in the Rocky Mountains* (1879) vividly recounts the dangers in winter as she rode on horseback through blizzards, her eyes frozen shut. In 1878 she traveled to Japan and stopped to visit Hong Kong, the Malay Peninsula, and Egypt on the way home.

Her sister Henrietta, with whom she lived on the Isle of Mull, was now gravely ill and being nursed by Dr. John Bishop, a close family friend. Bishop had previously proposed to Isabella, and six months after Henrietta died in June 1880, she finally agreed to marry him. She was fifty, and he was ten years her junior. He died five years later.

Three years after his death, Isabella Bishop went to India, where she established hospitals in memory of her sister and husband. During a two-month houseboat and horseback trip to Kashmir, which included visits to Tibetan monasteries, she broke several ribs as she was pulled from a flooding river. Next she agreed to allow a major in the Indian army to escort her across Persia. Hooded and covered like a Muslim woman, Bishop spent forty-six frigid days traveling with the group by saddle mule from Baghdad

■ *After a difficult journey from Baghdad to Tehran, Isabella Bird Bishop assembled a caravan that included four mules, a horse, an interpreter, a cook, and two servants to travel northwest from Persia through Luristan and Kurdistan to the Black Sea. She used her medical supplies to treat the sick and wounded who invaded her camp at each stop.*

CPH 3C08073

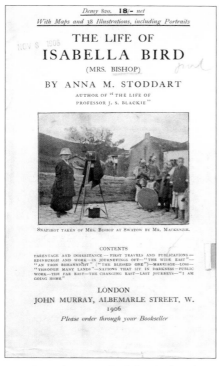

■ *At age sixty-three, Isabella Bird Bishop sailed again to East Asia and spent three years traveling in China, Korea, and Japan. During this eight-thousand-mile journey, much on the Yangtze River, she became adept at the new skill of photography and carried equipment to develop photographs.*

to Tehran. She wrote, "I never would have undertaken [the journey] had I known the hardships it would involve, the long marches, the wretched food, the abominable accommodation, the filthy water. . . ."

At age seventy, Bishop took a six-month trip to North Africa, where she rode with a companion through the Atlas Mountains on horseback. Exhausted by the trip, she returned to Edinburgh and died in October 1904.

DESERTS, JUNGLES, AND VILLAGES
WOMEN EXPLORE
INDIGENOUS CULTURES

UNLIKE IDA PFEIFFER and Isabella Bird Bishop, most women explorers did not have the means, time, desire, or stamina to spend years globe-trotting and chose instead to focus on specific regions. Women like Osa Johnson, Mary Hastings Bradley, and Delia Akeley found their calling after exploring lands in Africa and Asia with their husbands, although Akeley and Johnson later led their own expeditions. Other women spent their lives studying the culture, geography, and nature of particular places. They were recognized as experts, and their names—Gertrude Bell and Freya Stark in the Middle East, Louise Arner Boyd in eastern Greenland, and Mary Kingsley in West Africa—became synonymous with these regions. Two other women who revealed the secrets of foreign lands to readers at home were Harriet Chalmers Adams (South America) and Alexandra David-Néel (Tibet).

■ *After receiving a small inheritance, Englishwoman Mary Kingsley (1862–1900) journeyed alone to West Africa. On her arrival in Sierra Leone in August 1893, she traveled as a trader so she could easily move from village to village. During a second trip to Africa in 1894–1895, Kingsley lived with the cannibalistic Fang tribe; braved rapids in her canoe, snakes in the jungles, and crocodiles in the swamps; climbed the 13,435-foot Mount Cameroon; and became the first European to see Lake Ncovi. Her adventures were reported in the British press and earned her great fame.*
PHOTOGRAPH COURTESY ROYAL GEOGRAPHICAL SOCIETY

HARRIET CHALMERS ADAMS (1875–1937)

We all have a Mecca. . . . Since childhood I had journeyed in my dreams on the long pilgrimage to Cuzco [Peru], and when I at last found myself in the Andean country, on that portion of the old Inca highway stretching from Lake Titicaca to the "City of the Sun," I knew that sometimes dreams come true.

—Harriet Chalmers Adams, *National Geographic,* 1908

ADAMS WAS THE MOST PROLIFIC WOMAN ever to write for *National Geographic,* publishing twenty-one articles between 1907 and 1935. The first president of the Society of Woman Geographers and a member of numerous geographical societies throughout the world, she was called the "foremost woman explorer in this country" by *Who's Who in America.* As a war correspondent for *Harper's* magazine during World War I, she was the only female journalist permitted to visit the front lines in France. Yet, perhaps because she never wrote a book or because her vast photographic archive was destroyed in a flood, her contributions as an explorer have been overshadowed by others.

Born in Stockton, California, Adams said of her childhood, "Before I was fourteen, I had completed, on horseback, the entire Sierra Nevada Mountain chain with my father. He taught me to ride, shoot, swim, and fish. I never went to school after I was eleven, but I had private tutors in between trips in the saddle." She loved to read and was adept at learning languages: Spanish, Portuguese, Italian, French, and German. When she was fourteen her father took her on a yearlong ramble from Oregon to Mexico.

■ *"Living in California, as I did, in my girlhood, I had always been much interested in things of Spanish origin and influence. I was interested in South America too, from the time I used to hear my grandfather tell about the eventful days of '49, of how he and other men had sailed all the way around Cape Horn to reach the Pacific Coast. . . . I was thrilled to visit these same places and touch hands with the past, personal as well as historical."*
—*Harriet Chalmers Adams*

CPH 3B45568

From these early years on, Adams was gripped with a wanderlust that would take her to every former colony of Spain and Portugal, visiting every country in Central and South America, living among tribal people in the Philippines, Siberia, and Sumatra, and visiting every linguistic branch of the Indian tribes in the United States.

At twenty-four she married Franklin Pierce Adams and the next year accompanied him on an engineering survey trip to Mexico, where she fell in love with Latin America. Looking to continue their travels, her husband accepted a job in 1904 inspecting mines in Central and South America.

Harriet Adams had learned photography, and for the next three years they traveled by horseback, mule, dugout canoe, and boat while she amassed a huge collection of notes and over three thousand photographs.

In 1906, when the couple moved to Washington, DC, Adams approached the National Geographic Society with her research. Her first article, "Picturesque Paramaribo," was published in the Society's magazine in June 1907, illustrated by her photographs. At the Society's request, that December she delivered a lecture entitled "The Land of the Incas," which began her long and successful lecturing career.

From 1910 to 1912, she and her husband traveled to Cuba, Haiti (where she rode 510 miles by horse), Puerto Rico, and the Dominican Republic. After World War I, she continued her travels, often on her own, revisiting South America and researching in Spain and Morocco. In 1926 she fell off a seawall in the Balearic Islands and was rescued in the surf by Spanish fishermen. Her back was broken, and doctors predicted she would never walk again. She spent the next two years in a cast strapped to a board but eventually recovered. By 1928 she was off on a six-month trip to North Africa to complete her "firsthand knowledge of every country bordering the Mediterranean."

When Franklin Adams retired in 1934, they moved to Europe and spent the next two years traveling in the Balkans. Harriet Chalmers Adams died from kidney disease in southern France in July 1937.

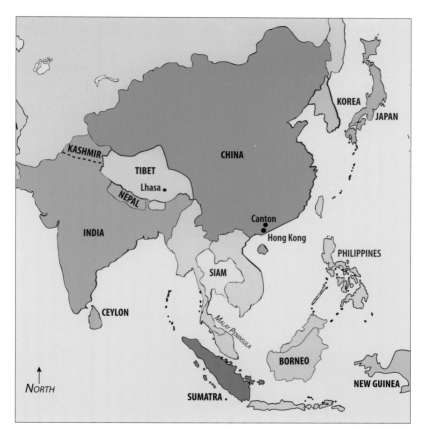

■ *Southeast Asia in the late 1800s. In 1913 Harriet Chalmers Adams traveled to the Philippines, Siberia, Mongolia, China, and Sumatra to study ancient races she thought may have migrated to the Americas. Before each trip, Adams read all available scientific literature and learned as much of the native languages as possible.*

MAP DESIGNED BY STEPHANIE HELLINE

SOCIETY OF WOMAN GEOGRAPHERS

. . . in a big expedition where the staff included a half dozen or more men I consider women to be a great detriment; they could not do a technical job in most cases any better than a man, and their sex alone made for complications. A leader has enough difficulties in running a big expedition without saddling himself with any that can be avoided.

—Roy Chapman Andrews, Explorers Club president, 1929

ALTHOUGH THE US NATIONAL GEOGRAPHIC SOCIETY, as well as geographic societies in many other countries, had bestowed membership on stellar female explorers, the Explorers Club, founded in New York City in 1904, did not admit women as members until the 1980s. In response, Marguerite Harrison, Blair Niles, Gertrude Shelby, and Gertrude Emerson Sen created the Society of Woman Geographers (SWG), also based in New York City, in 1925.

For women who had traveled extensively to investigate little-known places, people, and things, the SWG provided a forum in which they could share their experiences and encourage each other in future exploration and research. It included the related disciplines of anthropology, geology, biology, archaeology, oceanography, and ecology. As their first president, the founders selected Harriet Chalmers Adams, the most renowned American woman explorer of the day. Adams hosted the SWG in her home in Washington, DC, until 1931. Early SWG members credit

■ *An honor escort from the Society of Woman Geographers prepares to meet Amelia Earhart in 1932. A contributor to the January 26, 1927, issue of the* Christian Science Monitor *observed, "Certainly no clearer indication of the emancipation of women has been offered than the formation in 1926 of this group of explorers, archaeologists, botanists, ethnologists, and those of kindred natural sciences."*

PHOTOGRAPH COURTESY THE SOCIETY OF WOMAN GEOGRAPHERS

Adams' tireless promotion and enthusiasm with helping the organization grow from a handful of members to more than two hundred women in dozens of countries by 1933, when she resigned as president. And she accomplished this despite spending two years recovering from a broken back. Adams' dream for the SWG was "that it may some day be endowed and have a real home in Washington . . . , that it may become in time a

■ *Geologist, conservationist, and Society of Woman Geographers member Katharine Fowler Billings (1902–1997), second from right, and her entourage pose before walking the Grindelwald Glacier in 1922. Billings mapped the geology of the Laramie Mountains in Wyoming, several regions in New Hampshire, and Sierra Leone in Africa.*
PHOTOGRAPH COURTESY THE SOCIETY OF WOMAN GEOGRAPHERS AND THE BILLINGS FAMILY

world force to help young scientists understudy older ones, and that it may become a great international link between thinking, outstanding women of all nations."

Still headquartered in Washington, DC, the SWG has continued to grow. Since its inception, more than one thousand women have been members, including Rachel Carson, Amelia Earhart, Mary Leakey, and Margaret Mead. ■

ALEXANDRA DAVID-NÉEL (1868–1969)

Ever since I was five years old, a tiny precocious child of Paris, I wished to move out of the narrow limits in which . . . I was then kept. I craved to go beyond the garden gate, to follow the road that passed it by, and to set out for the unknown.

—Alexandra David-Néel

IN HER YOUTH Alexandra David-Néel, the only child of an unhappy couple, sought refuge in books and ran away from home a number of times. As a young woman she became interested in comparative religions and spent hours reading in the library of the Musée Guimet, a museum dedicated to Far Eastern antiquities. With a small inheritance from her godmother, she disobeyed her parents and traveled to India at age twenty-three to spend a year studying Indian philosophy and yoga. Needing money, she returned to Europe, found work as an opera singer, and began writing articles about Buddhism for "radical reviews." In 1904 she married Philippe-François Néel, an engineer she had met while performing in Tunis. But, as she explained to Philippe in her letters, she found the idea of traditional marriage with children stifling. A few days after the marriage she returned to Paris. He stayed in Tunis. For the next forty years they remained married but seldom lived together.

David-Néel became restless and depressed in the following years, so her husband paid for her to return to India in 1911. A year later, she became the first Western woman to be granted a private audience with the Dalai

■ *Alexandra David-Néel's trip to India in 1911 marked the beginning of her long and unusual relationship with her husband, Philippe. As she traveled for years through India, China, and Tibet, he continued to support her financially, transacted business for her, accepted her articles and had them typed and sent to designated journalists, and shipped her the supplies she needed.* MUSÉE ALEXANDRA DAVID-NÉEL

■ *Alexandra David-Néel's camp near Mount Kangchenjunga on the border between Nepal and Sikkim.* MUSÉE ALEXANDRA DAVID-NÉEL

Lama, then exiled in India. She moved to Sikkim to study Tibetan Buddhism, lectured about it throughout India, and learned the Tibetan language. She spent the winter of 1914–1915 living in a cave near a hermit who taught her about Tibetan customs. Driven to learn all she could about the mysteries of Tibetan Buddhism, she visited Nepal and illegally crossed into Tibet to visit several monasteries.

When she discovered the Indian government planned to deport her for her Tibetan incursion, David-Néel and Yongden, her assistant, took an extended tour of Burma, Japan, and China. In October 1917, as they arrived

■ *The Potala, palace of the Dalai Lama. After traveling for months through some of the harshest conditions on Earth, Alexandra David-Néel and Yongden, a student lama and her personal assistant, arrived in Lhasa. Until his death in France in 1957, Yongden would share all her travels and travails. She would be his teacher, and he would be the son she never had.* MUSÉE ALEXANDRA DAVID-NÉEL

in Peking, China was in the midst of a civil war, and travel was dangerous. They joined the caravan of a Tibetan lama and traveled by mule over two thousand miles in seven months to the Kumbum monastery. Here, among the three thousand resident monks, they settled in for the next three years while David-Néel busied herself translating ancient Buddhist texts.

For years she had been waiting for an opportunity to reenter Tibet and visit Lhasa, the seat of Tibetan Buddhism and home to the Dalai Lama. While a few westerners had been to Lhasa, many more were turned back by the authorities, killed by bandits, or had died from starvation or exposure in the harsh environment. In 1923 she hatched a plot that would not only let her realize this dream but also make her famous throughout the West. Traveling only with Yongden, now in his mid-twenties, she darkened her hair and face with ink, cocoa, and charcoal, lengthened her hair with yak braids, put on coarse clothing, and set off as an old Tibetan peasant with her son. They trudged through snow over mountain passes as high as eighteen thousand feet, slept out in the open and on dirt floors, and ate greasy food with peasant families. With little money, risking danger from the warring factions and discovery by Chinese authorities, she crossed one of the most rugged and remote landscapes on earth, much of it still unmapped.

In early 1924, they arrived in Lhasa where they visited the Potala palace, participated in religious ceremonies, and spent two months living among the Tibetan pilgrims. Via the letters she sent to her husband, David-Néel's amazing story preceded her return to Europe. When she arrived in France in May 1925, she was honored for her great contribution to the study of Tibetan culture. She received medals from geographical societies in France and Belgium and the rank of Knight in the French Legion of Honor. Her book *My Journey to Lhasa,* published in English and French in 1927, is one of the greatest adventure stories ever written and has never gone out of print.

In the next ten years, David-Néel wrote more books, including *Magic and Mystery in Tibet,* and was in constant demand to give lectures and write articles. Despite her husband's concern that Yongden would not adapt well to life in Europe, she convinced him to adopt the young man, who had returned with her to France.

In January 1936, fearing the changes she saw in pre–World War II Europe, David-Néel made the unfortunate decision to return to China with Yongden just as the Japanese were preparing to invade. In her letters to the president of the SWG in 1940, she describes her hardships:

> *When the Japanese war broke, I was near the Mongolian border. I have had to flee from place to place. I have been under air raids for months, met with accidents, have been wounded, lost my luggage. . . . the brigands roam across the country. Hardly one week elapses without one hearing of robbery on the roads, more than once the travelers are not only robbed but murdered.*

In January 1941, she learned that Philippe-François Néel had died. "I have lost the best of husbands and my only friend," she said later. After World War II, she returned to Europe and lived out her long life at Samten Dzong (Fortress of Meditation), her home in the south of France. She continued to write daily until a few weeks before her death in September 1969, shortly before her 101st birthday.

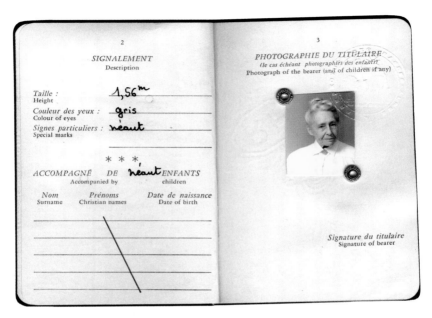

2

SIGNALEMENT
Description

Taille :
Height   1,56 m

Couleur des yeux :   gris
Colour of eyes

Signes particuliers :   néant
Special marks

* * *,

ACCOMPAGNÉ   DE néant ENFANTS
Accompanied by   children

Nom   Prénoms   Date de naissance
Surname   Christian names   Date of birth

3

PHOTOGRAPHIE DU TITULAIRE
(le cas échéant photographiés des enfants)
Photograph of the bearer (and of children if any)

Signature du titulaire
Signature of bearer

■ *At age one hundred, Alexandra David-Néel was promoted to the highest order of the French Legion of Honor, and she renewed her passport for a proposed trip to the United States.*
MUSÉE ALEXANDRA DAVID-NÉEL

■ *Between 1912 and 1936, Osa and Martin Johnson made numerous trips to Africa and Southeast Asia, filming many tribes and animals for the first time. She told an interviewer, "Even though I do what's usually considered a man's job, I always try to remain unmistakably feminine. I make up my face every morning of my life; it doesn't make any difference whether I'm going to stroll on Park Avenue or shoot some wild game for dinner. If my nose gets shiny in the middle of the day, I powder it—whether I've just shot a lion or just bought a dress or just finished baking a batch of pies."*

MARTIN AND OSA JOHNSON SAFARI MUSEUM, CHANUTE, KANSAS

OVERCOMING OBSTACLES: SOCIAL AND FAMILY LIFE

[T]o think of a woman's venturing alone, without protection of any kind, into the wide world, across sea and mountain and plain—it was quite preposterous. This was the opinion of my friends.

—Ida Pfeiffer, from *A Visit to the Holy Land, Egypt, and Italy* (1843)

DURING THE GOLDEN AGE OF EXPLORATION in the 1800s, a trip abroad meant traveling by ship and possibly train or carriage, so travelers could expect to be away from home for months, if not years. Well-funded men could afford to go exploring with large retinues, including family members, but for most women explorers, travel was not a family affair.

Women were expected to care for their children, aging parents, or ill relatives and rarely left their domestic responsibilities to travel. Thus long trips for personal pleasure became an option available only to the rare single woman or empty nester with money of her own, some education, strength and stamina, a natural curiosity, and a willingness to open herself to criticism.

So how were early women explorers able to spend months and years on the road? They were not afraid to travel alone, and, most importantly, they had limited, if any, family ties to keep them homebound. A number of well-known explorers—Mary Kingsley, Annie Smith Peck, Gertrude Bell, Louise Arner Boyd—never married. Some married women like

Alexandra David-Néel and Harriet Chalmers Adams had nontraditional, childless marriages that allowed them the flexibility to travel on their own. Isabella Bird Bishop and Freya Stark married late, at fifty and fifty-four respectively, after they had already traveled widely, and Bishop took some of her most celebrated journeys after her husband died.

Ida Pfeiffer began traveling in her forties after raising her sons and divorcing her husband. Fanny Bullock Workman and husband William began their years of exploration when they placed their daughter in a boarding school. Mary Hastings Bradley and husband Herbert took their five-year-old daughter with them to Africa in 1921. "That we took our child wasn't as mad as it seems," she told a reporter, "for we were going into the mountains . . . and separation from her was just unthinkable to us." But Bradley, who later wrote *Alice in Jungleland* based on her daughter's experience in Africa, was an exception.

As decades passed, people could travel more quickly and for less money. It became more commonplace to see women of all ages, with and without families, traveling to remote or dangerous areas. In the early 1970s mountaineer Junko Tabei trained for her attempt on Mount Everest while raising a young daughter with her husband. In 1987 explorer Arlene Blum hiked across the Alps from Yugoslavia to France carrying her infant daughter on her back. As modern-day British explorer Christina Dodwell has said, "In the past women had to break out of normal life to go traveling. Now they are considered incomplete if they have not ventured abroad." ■

■ *Freya Stark, by Herbert Olivier, oil on canvas, 1923. British explorer Dame Freya Stark (1893–1993) traveled to Lebanon and Syria when she was thirty-four, learned the local languages, and devoted her life to studying the Middle East. She eventually wrote more than twenty books. During World War II, she worked for Britain's Ministry of Information in Aden and Egypt, encouraging the Arabs to support the Allies. At eighty-seven she journeyed on horseback for three weeks in Nepal with a friend and sherpas. They rode seven to eight hours a day "with no purpose except pure enjoyment."*

NATIONAL PORTRAIT GALLERY, LONDON. NPG 5465

ON TOP OF THE WORLD
WOMEN EXPLORE THE
HIGHEST PEAKS

MODERN MOUNTAIN CLIMBING became popular in the mid-nineteenth century as European adventurers raced to the top of one Alpine peak after another. Several adventurous women participated in this craze early on: in 1808 Frenchwoman Marie Paradis climbed Mont Blanc, the highest peak in western Europe, and in 1871 British climber Lucy Walker successfully scaled the Matterhorn (14,691 ft.), the most challenging peak in Europe. While the world's first mountaineering club, the Alpine Club (London, 1857) refused to admit women, the US Appalachian Mountain Club (Boston, 1876) accepted and encouraged women to enjoy "tramping," as hiking was then called. In New Hampshire women worked with men to explore, map, and build trails in the White Mountains. Around the turn of the century, two Americans, Annie Smith Peck and Fanny Bullock Workman, took women's mountain climbing to greater heights while also collecting valuable scientific data.

ANNIE SMITH PECK (1850–1935)

ANNIE SMITH PECK'S early years gave no indication that, after age forty-five, her life would take a turn that would lead her to found the American Alpine Club, become a member in the Royal Geographical Society and the SWG, and find fame, if not exactly fortune. Peck was very well educated.

■ *In the 1890s, most women still wore skirts when they hiked or climbed mountains. By climbing the Matterhorn in pants, Annie Smith Peck became a celebrity. Singer Sewing Machine Company even included this photograph of Peck in her climbing gear with every new machine they sold.*

CPH 3C18273

She trained as a teacher at Rhode Island State Normal School and then attended the University of Michigan, one of the few universities open to women. After graduating with honors in 1878, she received her master's degree in Greek and became one of the first female college professors in the United States, teaching Latin and elocution at Purdue University.

While on a study trip in Europe in 1885, she caught her first glimpse of the Matterhorn. "On beholding this majestic, awe-inspiring peak," she later wrote, "I felt that I should never be happy until I, too, should scale those frowning walls which have beckoned so many upwards, a few to their own destruction." Back in the United States, between teaching and lecturing on Roman and Greek archaeology, Peck began climbing small mountains, eventually tackling her first big peak, Mount Shasta (14,162 ft.) in California, in 1888.

When Peck successfully climbed the Matterhorn in 1895, she was only the third woman to do it. In 1897 she climbed Pico de Orizaba (18,700 ft.) and Popocatépetl (17,887 ft.) in Mexico. Yet despite these successes and the overly sensationalized newspaper stories that covered them, she spent the next four years trying to raise funds to scale what she thought to be the highest peak in the Western Hemisphere, the unclimbed Mount Sorata (now called Illampu) in Bolivia.

In 1903, when she finally had enough money, she hired two Swiss guides, an American professor, and Bolivian porters. Unfortunately, her guides were unreliable and argumentative, and her porters refused to go on when the going got tough. After two unsuccessful attempts on Sorata, she turned her attention in 1904 to the twin-peaked Mount Huascarán in Peru,

■ *In 1908 Annie Smith Peck hired two Swiss guides and traveled to Peru by ship. In this image, they carry ice axes and some of the photographic and scientific equipment she took on her expeditions to measure altitude, atmospheric pressure, and humidity.* GGBAIN 01980

which she now knew to be higher. It took her four years and six attempts, but on September 1, 1908, Annie Smith Peck became the first person to summit Huascarán Norte (21,812 ft.)—which Peru later named Cumbre Aña Peck in her honor—and the first woman to make the initial ascent of a major peak. Two years later she reached the north summit of the unclimbed 21,000-foot Mount Coropuna in Peru and planted a "Votes for Women" sign at the top.

Peck had always hoped that her focus on South American peaks would lead North Americans to take a greater interest in their neighbors to the south. To this end, she began her last great adventure in 1929 at the age of eighty: a seven-month tour of South America by air. Air routes were just being established in many places, but she sought them out, crisscrossing the entire continent and the Caribbean, photographing and taking extensive notes. The planes, often small, occasionally had to make emergency landings, but Peck journeyed on, capturing the entire tale in her book *Flying Over South America: Twenty Thousand Miles by Air*.

She died in July 1935 in New York City after a short illness.

Fanny Bullock Workman (1859–1925)

FANNY BULLOCK, the daughter of a Massachusetts governor, was born into a wealthy family. Like other girls in her social class, she was tutored privately and attended a finishing school for young women. At age twenty-two, after spending two years studying in France and Germany, she returned home and married William Workman, a thirty-four-year-old physician. Three years later they had their only child, Rachel.

For a time they lived
in New England, where
William introduced Fanny
to hiking in the White Mountains. When poor health forced
William to give up his practice, the couple moved to Europe in 1889 and
began their years of traveling and mountaineering in earnest. After placing
Rachel in boarding school, they got swept up in the bicycling craze and
cycled through Spain and North Africa, then pedaled across India and
Southeast Asia. The three books they wrote about their bicycling experiences, featuring photos by Fanny, all sold well.

■ *"[W]e had breathed the atmosphere of that great mountain-world, had drunk of the swirling waters of its glaciers, and feasted our eyes on the incomparable beauty and majesty of its towering peaks, and, as time passed on, its charms asserted their power anew and called to us with irresistible siren strains to return yet once again to those regions. . . ." —Fanny Bullock Workman, on returning to the Karakoram Range*

In 1898, to escape the heat in India, the Workmans ventured north into the Himalayas of Kashmir and were smitten. The following year they decided to focus on the Karakoram, the mountains to the west of the Himalayas, which contained many unexplored peaks and glaciers. Over the next fourteen years, they organized six expeditions to this region. Whenever possible, they worked with Britain's Great Trigonometrical Survey of India. The couple wrote five books detailing their high-altitude adventures.

In 1899, Fanny Workman set a women's altitude record by climbing the 21,000-foot Mount Koser Gunge. Her 1906 ascent of Pinnacle Peak (22,810 ft.) in the Nun Kun massif remained a women's record for twenty-eight years.

During the Workmans' final expedition, as they traversed the 45-mile-long Siachen Glacier, one of their porters fell through the ice and died. Their decision—reached after much soul-searching—to continue the expedition allowed them to discover a wholly unknown region in the mountains and eventually write the book that would be their greatest contribution to science: *Two Summers in the Ice-Wilds of Eastern Karakoram* (1917).

Fanny Bullock Workman was proud of the credentials and citations she collected over the years, despite what she saw as efforts by some men to discredit her work. She was a fellow of the Royal Geographical Society and the Royal Scottish Geographical Society, the recipient of medals from ten other geographic societies, a member of numerous alpine clubs, the first American woman to lecture at the Sorbonne, and the second woman ever (after Isabella Bird Bishop) to lecture at the Royal Geographical Society. She died at age sixty-five in Cannes, France, after a long illness.

JUNKO TABEI (B. 1939)

SEVEN DECADES after Fanny Bullock Workman climbed the Nun Kun massif, many people still believed that women were not made to climb mountains. Japanese mountaineer Junko Tabei dispelled that notion on May 16, 1975, when she became the first woman to climb the world's highest peak, Mount Everest (29,035 ft.). Tabei, who began climbing mountains when she was ten, had founded the Japanese Ladies Climbing Club in 1969, when men's climbing clubs would not accept women. She spent three years training for her ascent of Everest while raising money for the trip and her all-female team. During the climb, an avalanche injured several team members, including Tabei, and destroyed some of their equipment. In the end, only Tabei and Sherpa Ang Tshering reached the peak.

■ *Junko Tabei on the summit of Mount Everest, 1975. In 1992, the four-foot-nine Tabei became the first woman to climb the Seven Summits, the highest mountain on each continent. She later founded the Himalayan Adventure Trust of Japan to protect and clean up mountain environments around the globe.*
ASSOCIATED PRESS

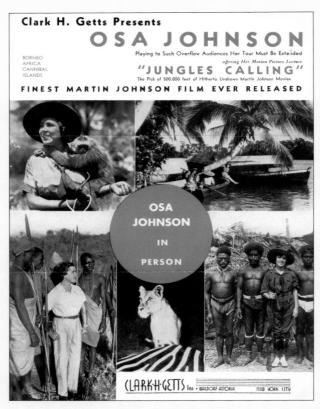

Clark H. Getts Presents

OSA JOHNSON

Playing to Such Overflow Audiences Her Tour Must Be Extended

BORNEO
AFRICA
CANNIBAL
ISLANDS

offering Her Motion Picture Lecture

"JUNGLES CALLING"

The Pick of 500,000 feet of Hitherto Unshown Martin Johnson Movies

FINEST MARTIN JOHNSON FILM EVER RELEASED

OSA
JOHNSON
IN
PERSON

CLARK·H·GETTS Inc · WALDORF-ASTORIA   NEW YORK CITY

■ *In 1937 Osa Johnson (1894–1953) was severely injured in the plane crash that killed Martin, her husband. In addition to her collaborative work with Martin, she later produced one film (*Jungles Calling*) and wrote four books on her own.*

REDPATH CHAUTAUQUA COLLECTION, UNIVERSITY OF IOWA LIBRARIES, IOWA

OVERCOMING OBSTACLES:
FINANCING A JOURNEY

BEFORE WORLD WAR II, women explorers did not have access to large grants from governments, museums, or geographic societies, and few women had money of their own. Since financing affected every aspect of their travels, women had to find ways to fund their expeditions.

Early explorers Ida Pfeiffer, Isabella Bird Bishop, and Mary Kingsley all inherited small sums from their parents, which they used to begin their travels. They later earned money for future trips by writing books or giving lectures—the most consistent sources of money for women explorers. Some married women, such as Harriet Chalmers Adams, Osa Johnson, and Mary Hastings Bradley, initially traveled with their husbands on business but later lectured and wrote books to earn additional income. Alexandra David-Néel's husband funded her extended trips to Asia before her books sold well enough to support her. A few fortunate women like Gertrude Bell, Louise Arner Boyd, May French Sheldon, and Fanny Bullock Workman were born wealthy and could self-fund their journeys.

The vastly different financial circumstances of two renowned female mountain climbers, Annie Smith Peck and Fanny Bullock Workman, greatly influenced their expeditions. Peck, neither wealthy nor married, spent years trying to raise money to fund her ventures to Mexico and South America. The money she raised by selling her story to newspapers, lecturing, and asking advertisers for $100 contributions often barely covered her expenses. If anything went wrong—and it usually did—she

HARRIET CHALMERS ADAMS

Explorer - Lecturer

is sailing for the Far East to lecture and gather Travel Story material

Mrs. Adams will be available for lecture engagements in U. S. A. after January 1st, 1914.

For terms and open time, address Charles M. Cousins, 917 Eighteenth Street, N. W., Washington, D. C., on and after October 15th, 1913.

MASONIC TEMPLE AUDITORIUM
NEXT SATURDAY EVENING, MARCH 18
HARRIET CHALMERS ADAMS, F. R. G. S.

Will deliver her lecture on **"Rondonia in the Brazilian Wilderness,"** illustrated by colored slides and five reels of marvelous motion pictures recently made on the Roosevelt Trail, through the heart of South America.

From the Paraguay to the Madeira; Slaying the Mighty Jaguar; Unique Game of Head-Ball; Jungle People in Jungle Dances; Rafting Rubber to the Amazon.

For the past eleven seasons Mrs. Adams has appeared in the lecture course of the National Geographic Society.

This March 18 lecture is open to the public. Tickets $1.10, including war tax, now on sale at 1306 G Street, T. Arthur Smith, Inc.

■ *For her lectures, the five-foot-tall Harriet Chalmers Adams would often wear a long red evening gown and show color slides, a first in the Western Hemisphere, while she entertained the crowd with thrilling tales of the exotic people and places she had visited.*

MANUSCRIPT DIVISION, LIBRARY OF CONGRESS

had to abandon her mission and return to New York for another round of fund-raising. In contrast, Workman and her husband were able to finance their own trips. They could afford to ship their equipment from England to India and hire the necessary porters and guides. Because they had the requisite funding, they had more time to plan, more time to explore and

■ *Wealthy American May French Sheldon (1847–1936) financed and led her first expedition to east Africa in 1891. Upon her return, she wrote articles for scholarly journals and lectured at professional societies in Europe and the United States. Her book* Sultan to Sultan, *which contained new anthropological information about the women and children she had met, was considered a notable contribution to geography and ethnography.*

Circumnavigation of Lake Chala.

FROM NATIVE SULTAN TO SULTAN

AMONG THE MASAI AND OTHER TRIBES IN EAST AFRICA.

Mrs. M. FRENCH-SHELDON

(Bébé Bwana)

AUTHOR AND AFRICAN EXPLORER,

Will Deliver her first Lecture in Washington, D. C., for the National Geographical Society,

AT

BUILDERS' EXCHANGE HALL,

Friday Evening, May 20, at 8 o'clock,

Illustrated by Original Lantern Slides, and many Unique Curios from known Unique Collections.

* Sultan to Sultan. My Adventures among the Masai and other Native Tribes of East Africa, by M. French-Sheldon (Bébé Bwana). In press. Arena Publishing Co., Boston, Mass.

map, and a much larger traveling party—rare luxuries for a woman explorer.

Women explorers today can compete more successfully against their male counterparts for grants, though many must still self-fund their expeditions. Mountaineer Arlene Blum partly financed her 1978 all-woman expedition to Annapurna by selling T-shirts emblazoned with "A Woman's

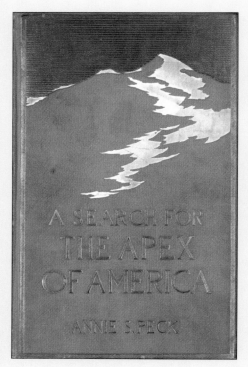

"Place Is on Top." For her trek across the Himalayas, she and her partner received their gear and clothing free from retailer L. L. Bean. Other explorers like Helen Thayer, Christina Dodwell, and Ann Bancroft rely on book sales, speaker's fees, and, increasingly, sponsorships from major corporations for income. ■

AT THE EDGES OF THE EARTH
WOMEN EXPLORE
THE POLAR REGIONS

LOUISE ARNER BOYD (1887–1972)

IN 1924, A SAN FRANCISCO heiress and socialite journeyed to the Arctic on a tourist cruise that would change her life. After her trip to Spitsbergen, Louise Arner Boyd wrote:

Far north, hidden behind grim barriers of pack ice, are lands that hold one spellbound. Gigantic imaginary gates . . . seem to guard these lands. The gates swing open, and one enters another world where men are insignificant amid the awesome immensity of lovely mountains, fiords, and glaciers.

■ *In 1939, after six trips to the Arctic, Louise Arner Boyd said in a radio broadcast, "Most people imagine that the polar regions are dreary areas, perpetually covered with ice and snow. But many parts of the far north that I have visited have a beauty not found anywhere else in the world."*

CPH 3C19368

51

What Boyd saw and felt on this trip would compel her to divide the next twenty-five years of her life between social events at home and months spent onboard ships above the Arctic Circle photographing and mapping the east coast of Greenland.

She became famous in 1928 when she lent her crew, equipment, and rented boat to the Norwegian government to search for missing polar explorer Roald Amundsen and his party. Boyd and her ship joined Norwegian, French, Russian, and Italian vessels in the unsuccessful attempt to find Amundsen. Newspapers across the United States covered the search and the American woman who was helping out. That summer she took thousands of photos and shot twenty thousand feet of film—a vocation she continued passionately on future expeditions.

Boyd eventually planned and paid for seven expeditions to the Arctic, taking with her handpicked botanists, geologists, hydrographers, and surveyors. She also brought the most modern scientific equipment to study plant and animal life, photograph and map the extensive fiords of eastern Greenland, and measure sea depths between Norway and Greenland. In 1931 she discovered an unknown glacier, and in 1933 her expedition mapped in detail the inner reaches of the Ice Fiord. For her scientific contribution, Denmark named the region Miss Boyd Land. On a later expedition, her team discovered an unknown underwater mountain range.

She had a long and mutually beneficial collaboration with the American Geographical Society. In 1935 they published *The Fiord Region of East Greenland,* which she coauthored with five scientists. In 1938 the Society awarded her the Cullum Geographical Medal, its highest honor.

As World War II began, Boyd turned over the reports, photos, and

maps of her previous expeditions to the US Army, which was concerned about weather stations the Germans were building in Greenland. At the army's request, she postponed publishing her second book, *The Coast of Northeast Greenland,* until 1948. As a consultant to the National Bureau of Standards, she headed a 1941 Arctic expedition to collect data on the conditions of the ionosphere that could affect long-distance radio transmissions; she chartered the ship and paid all expenses herself. Throughout the war, she served as an unpaid advisor on Greenland and Spitsbergen to the Department of War. The army later awarded her a certificate of appreciation for "outstanding patriotic service to the Department of the Army as a contributor of geographic knowledge and as a consultant during the critical months immediately before and after the start of World War II."

In 1955, at age sixty-eight, Louise Arner Boyd chartered a plane to fly from Norway over the North Pole—the first nonmilitary flight over the pole and the first time a woman had flown over it. She died in 1972, and her ashes were scattered over the Arctic as she had requested.

LATER POLAR EXPEDITIONS

IN 1986 AMERICAN POLAR EXPLORER Ann Bancroft became the first known woman to reach the North Pole over the ice when she traveled a thousand miles by dogsled from Canada with the Steger International Polar Expedition. Two years later, New Zealander Helen Thayer became the first woman to travel to the magnetic north pole—alone and unsupported. During her twenty-seven-day trek with her dog Charlie, Thayer walked and skied 364 miles, pulling a sled loaded with 160 pounds of supplies. She was fifty years old at the time.

■ ABOVE: *In 1994 Norwegian Liv Arnesen (b. 1953) spent fifty days traveling 745 miles to become the first woman to ski solo to the South Pole, completely unsupported. In 2001, Arnesen joined American Ann Bancroft (b. 1955) and together they spent ninety-four days sailing and skiing the 1,717 miles across Antarctica's landmass.*

PHOTOGRAPH COURTESY BANCROFT ARNESEN EXPLORE, WWW.BANCROFTARNESENEXPLORE.COM

■ LEFT: *Helen Thayer's career has been marked by her long treks, with and without her husband Bill, studying high- and low-altitude deserts, wolves in the Canadian Yukon, and caribou on the North Slope of Alaska. In 1996 she became the first woman to walk across the Sahara Desert following an ancient 2,400-mile camel trade route. The very next year she walked 450 miles alone in Antarctica, pulling a 260-pound sled. In 2002 the National Geographic Society named Thayer "One of the Great Explorers of the 20th Century."* PHOTOGRAPH COURTESY HELEN THAYER

OVERCOMING OBSTACLES: THE RIGHT ATTIRE AND EQUIPMENT

WHEN ISABELLA BIRD BISHOP left for Australia in 1872, England and the United States were in the throes of a dress reform movement that would eventually lead to women wearing more practical and comfortable clothing. But decades would pass before women put aside their corsets, laced petticoats, and long, heavy dresses to wear looser-fitting undergarments, bloomers, and divided skirts. As women like Bishop decided what to wear while traveling through jungles, up mountains, and across deserts, each chose clothing that gave her the level of comfort she found necessary to travel solo in strange lands and challenging situations.

■ *May French Sheldon wore an elaborate silk ball gown and blond wig to meet important tribesmen on her African expeditions "as a woman of breeding should meet the highest officials in any land, under any circumstances, and be civil and polite for favors granted."*
GENERAL COLLECTIONS, LIBRARY OF CONGRESS

■ *Mary Kingsley's ever-present sealskin hat. Although a fearless traveler and independent woman, Kingsley was no suffragist and even argued against women being given the vote in British parliamentary elections. She had similarly conservative views about dress, which she expressed in* Travels In West Africa: *"As for encasing the more earthward extremities of my anatomy in trousers, I would rather have perished on a scaffold."*
PHOTOGRAPH COURTESY ROYAL GEOGRAPHICAL SOCIETY

■ *Raised in Geneva by nonconformists and educated in numerous languages and sciences, twenty-year-old Isabelle Eberhardt (1877–1904) converted to Islam, as did her mother. In 1900 she moved to Algeria, where she led the life of a desert nomad. She could speak and write Arabic fluently, drank heavily, smoked hashish, and traveled about dressed as a man in Arab society.*

Many Victorian-era women opted to travel in the same long skirts with tight waistlines they wore at home. No matter where they set their bags down, they saw themselves as women of a certain status and felt obligated to dress appropriately. Mary Kingsley, traveling alone with her native guides in West Africa, always wore a high-necked white blouse, long black wool skirt, buttoned leather boots, and sealskin hat. She always carried her umbrella. Swiss writer and explorer Isabelle Eberhardt took an opposite approach: she frequently traveled through North Africa dressed in men's clothing.

Ardent women's rights supporter Fanny Bullock Workman refused to wear trousers, divided skirts, or bloomers when cycling or hiking, preferring floor-length skirts, long-sleeved blouses, and a hat with a veil. On later hikes, she wore slightly shorter skirts (mid-calf) and leggings. Annie Smith Peck, however, refused to wear a skirt while climbing mountains and shocked the public by famously climbing the Matterhorn in knickerbockers, a hip-length woolen tunic, leather leggings, and a felt hat tied with a veil.

These women did not have access to specialized equipment and clothing. Mountain climbers of the time pounded nails through the bottom of leather boots to create the primitive crampons needed to trek on snow and ice. At altitudes up to twenty-two thousand feet, Peck's warmest piece of clothing was Arctic explorer Robert Peary's animal-skin parka, lent to her by the American Museum of Natural History. (This parka was lost during her fourth attempt on Peru's Mount Huascarán when a porter let it fall into a crevasse.)

Travelers in cold climates wore layers of wool and tweed clothing, which became leaden when wet. Sleeping bags were made from army blankets, canvas, or camel hair and could be measured in pounds not ounces. Explorers had no small cameras, compact equipment, or dehydrated food to lighten the load.

Manufacturers today offer synthetic clothing, smaller-frame backpacks, and sleeping bags designed specifically for women, and some companies have made their mark by specializing solely in athletic and adventure clothing for women. ∎

■ *From her first trip in 1892 until her death in Baghdad in 1926, university-educated Gertrude Bell traveled extensively throughout the Middle East. Fluent in Arabic and Persian, she met with Arab chieftains, supervised archaeological expeditions, and served as advisor to Faisal I, the first ruler of Iraq. Yet this adventurous woman was also secretary of the Women's National Anti-Suffrage League in England.*

PHOTOGRAPH COURTESY UNIVERSITY OF NEWCASTLE UPON TYNE

■ *"Getting dressed that morning was relatively easy, as I had slept in my regular underwear, my long underwear, a cotton turtleneck, wool sweater, down vest, heavy down parka, wool pants, down pants, two hats, face mask, wool mittens, and two pairs of socks. Finally I put on my windbreaker, wind pants, boots, outer mittens, and daypack and then strapped metal crampons onto my feet."*
—American explorer Dr. Arlene Blum (b. 1960), describing a high-altitude morning
PHOTOGRAPH COURTESY ARLENE BLUM

EXPLORATION IN THE
TWENTY-FIRST CENTURY

IN THE TWENTY-FIRST CENTURY, we are no longer surprised to find women oceanographers, pilots, physicists, archaeologists, engineers, and astronauts on the frontiers of exploration, researching the seas, the cosmos, the smallest particles in the universe. Today more women than ever are drawn to travel and research—women who look at a mountain, an ocean, or a star and feel a special connection, an often indescribable pull to see and learn everything they can about the object of their passion. These women are willing to take calculated risks to fulfill their dreams and devote their lives to bringing new knowledge to the rest of us.

■ *Argentinean high-altitude archaeologist Dr. Constanza Ceruti climbing Aconcagua (22,841 ft.), the highest mountain in the Western Hemisphere. Ceruti (b. 1973) combines her interest in mountaineering with her academic training in archaeology to search for Incan ceremonial centers high in the Andes. On the summit of volcano Llullaillaco (22,100 ft.)—the site of the highest archaeological work ever undertaken—she and Dr. Johan Reinhard discovered three of the best-preserved mummies in the world.*

PHOTOGRAPH COURTESY
CONSTANZA CERUTI

■ *British explorer Christina Dodwell (b. 1951), seen here with a warrior-friend in Papua New Guinea, has written nine books on her travels in China, Siberia, Madagascar, New Guinea, Africa, eastern Turkey, and Iran. She has also made three films for television and numerous radio documentaries for the BBC.* PHOTOGRAPH COURTESY CHRISTINA DODWELL

As Helen Thayer (b. 1938) said recently, "Women of my generation who have dared to go forth have paved the way for the younger women coming along and they will pave the way for future generations. We build on each other." ■

■ *American writer and adventurer Dr. Kira Salak (b. 1971) was the first documented person to kayak solo six hundred miles down the Niger River to Timbuktu in Mali and the first woman to traverse Papua New Guinea. She has traveled alone on bicycle, horse, and foot in some of the most remote regions left on Earth. She says, "Ever since I was a child when someone tells me I can't do something, it just empowers me all the more. People's doubts in my ability only strengthen my resolve."*

PHOTOGRAPH © REMI BENALI

■ *A member of Arlene Blum's 1976 Everest expedition on a ladder bridging an enormous crevasse above Mount Everest Camp I.*

PHOTOGRAPH COURTESY ARLENE BLUM

FURTHER READING AND SOURCES

BOOKS BY EXPLORERS

Arnesen, Liv, Ann Bancroft, and Cheryl Dahle. *No Horizon Is So Far: Two Women and Their Historic Journey Across Antarctica*. New York: Penguin, 2004.

Bird [Bishop], Isabella L. *A Lady's Life in the Rocky Mountains*. 1879. Reprint, Whitefish, MT: Kessinger, 2004.

———. *Unbeaten Tracks in Japan*. 1880. Reprint, Whitefish, MT: Kessinger, 2004.

Blum, Arlene. *Annapurna: A Woman's Place*. 20th anniversary ed. San Francisco: Sierra Club Books, 1998.

David-Néel, Alexandra. *My Journey to Lhasa*. 1927. Reprint, New York: Harper Perennial, 2005.

Dodwell, Christina. *In Papua New Guinea*. 1983. Reprinted as *Travels in Papua New Guinea* by Long Riders' Guild Press, 2005.

Pfeiffer, Ida. *Visit to Iceland and the Scandinavian North*. 1852. Reprint, Lititz, PA: BiblioBazaar, 2006.

———. *A Woman's Journey Round the World*. 1854. Reprint, Whitefish, MT: Kessinger, 2004.

Salak, Kira. *Four Corners: A Journey into the Heart of Papua New Guinea*. 2001. Reprint, Washington, DC: National Geographic Society, 2004.

Thayer, Helen. *Polar Dream: The First Solo Expedition by a Woman and Her Dog to the Magnetic North Pole*. Troutdale, OR: New Sage Press, 2002.

Workman, Fanny Bullock, and William Hunter Workman. *The Call of the Snowy Hispar*. 1910. Reprint, Boston: Elibron Classics, 2002.

BOOKS ABOUT EXPLORERS

Anema, Durlynn. *Harriet Chalmers Adams: Adventurer and Explorer*. 2nd ed. Aurora, CO: National Writers Press, 2004.

Birkett, Dea. *Spinsters Abroad: Victorian Lady Explorers*. New York: Dorset Press, 1989.

Brown, Rebecca A. *Women on High: Pioneers of Mountaineering*. Boston: Appalachian Mountain Club Books, 2002.

Foster, Barbara, and Michael Foster. *Forbidden Journey: The Life of Alexandra David-Néel*. San Francisco: Harper & Row, 1987.

Miller, Luree. *On Top of the World: Five Women Explorers in Tibet*. New York: Paddington Press, 1976.

Olds, Elizabeth Fagg. *Women of the Four Winds*. Boston: Houghton Mifflin, 1985.

Polk, Milbry, and Mary Tiegreen. *Women of Discovery: A Celebration of Intrepid Women Who Explored the World*. New York: Clarkson Potter, 2001.

Slung, Michele. *Living With Cannibals and Other Women's Adventures*. Washington, DC: National Geographic Society, 2000.

Tinling, Marion. *Women into the Unknown: A Sourcebook on Women Explorers and Travelers*. New York: Greenwood Press, 1989.

ACKNOWLEDGMENTS

The author would like to thank contemporary explorers Liv Arnesen, Ann Bancroft, Arlene Blum, Constanza Ceruti, Christina Dodwell, Kira Salak, and Helen Thayer for participating in this project and inspiring her almost beyond words; series editor Amy Pastan for her hard work and steady guidance; Susan Reyburn, Laurie Stahl, Janet McGinn of the Society of Woman Geographers, Anne Atwood, Tammy Wong, and Stephanie Helline for their invaluable assistance; the Library of Congress' Publishing Office staff; and, especially, Athena Angelos for helping her to be in the right place at the right time.

IMAGES

Reproduction numbers, when available, are given for all items in the collections of the Library of Congress. Unless otherwise noted, Library of Congress images are from the Prints and Photographs Division. To order reproductions, note the number provided with the image; where no number exists, note the Library division and the title of the item. Direct your request to:

The Library of Congress
Photoduplication Service
Washington DC 20540-4570
(202) 707-5640; www.loc.gov